Python Descriptors

Understanding and Using the Descriptor Protocol

Second Edition

Jacob Zimmerman

Apress®

Python Descriptors: Understanding and Using the Descriptor Protocol

Jacob Zimmerman
New York, USA

ISBN-13 (pbk): 978-1-4842-3726-7   ISBN-13 (electronic): 978-1-4842-3727-4
https://doi.org/10.1007/978-1-4842-3727-4

Library of Congress Control Number: 2018960194

Managing Director, Apress Media LLC: Welmoed Spahr
Acquisitions Editor: Steve Anglin
Development Editor: Matthew Moodie
Coordinating Editor: Mark Powers

Cover designed by eStudioCalamar

Cover image designed by Freepik (www.freepik.com)

Distributed to the book trade worldwide by Springer Science+Business Media New York, 233 Spring Street, 6th Floor, New York, NY 10013. Phone 1-800-SPRINGER, fax (201) 348-4505, e-mail orders-ny@springer-sbm.com, or visit www.springeronline.com. Apress Media, LLC is a California LLC and the sole member (owner) is Springer Science + Business Media Finance Inc (SSBM Finance Inc). SSBM Finance Inc is a **Delaware** corporation.

For information on translations, please e-mail editorial@apress.com; for reprint, paperback, or audio rights, please email bookpermissions@springernature.com.

Apress titles may be purchased in bulk for academic, corporate, or promotional use. eBook versions and licenses are also available for most titles. For more information, reference our Print and eBook Bulk Sales web page at http://www.apress.com/bulk-sales.

Any source code or other supplementary material referenced by the author in this book is available to readers on GitHub via the book's product page, located at www.apress.com/9781484237267. For more detailed information, please visit http://www.apress.com/source-code.

Printed on acid-free paper

Table of Contents

About the Author

Jacob Zimmerman is a blogger, gamer (tabletop more so than video games), and programmer who was born and raised in Wisconsin. He has a twin brother who could also be considered to have all those traits.

Jacob has his own programming blog that focuses on Java, Kotlin, and Python programming, called "Programming Ideas with Jake". He also writes for a gaming blog with his brother-in-law called the "Ramblings of Jacob and Delos".

His brother writes a JavaScript blog called JoeZimJS and works with his best friend on a gaming YouTube channel called "Bork & Zim Gaming," which Jacob helps out with on occasion.

Programming Ideas with Jake

`http://programmingideaswithjake.wordpress.com/`

Ramblings of Jacob and Delos

`http://www.ramblingsofjacobanddelos.com/`

JoeZimJS

`http://www.joezimjs.com`

About the Technical Reviewer

Michael Thomas has worked in software development for more than 20 years as an individual contributor, team lead, program manager, and vice president of engineering. Michael has more than 10 years of experience working with mobile devices. His current focus is in the medical sector, using mobile devices to accelerate information transfer between patients and health care providers.

Acknowledgments

In order to be sure that I got everything right—it would really suck for a "comprehensive guide" to be missing a big chunk of functionality or to get anything wrong—I enlisted the help of some Python experts on the first edition. In return for their help, I let them introduce themselves to you here. That's not all I did in return, but it's all you're going to see :)

Emanuel Barry is a self-taught Python programmer who loves pushing the language to its limits as well as exploring its darkest corners. He has to do a lot of proofreading and editing for a local non-for-profit organization, and decided to combine his love of Python and knowledge sharing with his background in proofreading to help make this book even better. He can often be found in the shadows of the mailing lists or the issue tracker, as well as the Python IRC channel, as Vgr.

Chris Angelico has played around with Python since the late 90s, getting more serious with the language in the mid 2000s. As a PEP Editor and active participant in the various mailing lists, he keeps well up to date with what's new and upcoming in the language and also shares that knowledge with fledgling students in the Thinkful tutoring/mentoring program. When not coding in Python, he is often found wordsmithing for a Dungeons & Dragons campaign, or exploring the linguistic delights of Alice in Wonderland and similar works. If you find a subtle Alice reference in this text, blame him!

https://github.com/Rosuav

Kevin Mackay is a software engineer who has been programming in Python since 2010 and is currently working at BBC, improving the Taster platform. He is enthusiastic about open source software and occasionally contributes to the 3D graphics application, Blender. He can be found on the Python IRC channel as yakca or hiking on a mountain somewhere in Scotland.

Introduction

Python is a remarkable language with many surprisingly powerful features baked into it. Generators, metaclasses, and decorators are some of those, but this book is all about descriptors.

Code Samples

All code samples are written in Python 3, since that is the most recent version, but all the ideas and principles taught in this book apply to Python 2 as well, as long as you're using new style classes.

The Descriptor Tools Library

Written alongside this book was a library, called descriptor-tools, which can be installed with pip. It contains the fruition of a lot of the ideas and helpers to make it easier to implement them all. It's an open source project with a public GitHub repository.[1]

Note Superscript letters like the one at the end of the previous line are in reference to the bibliography at the back of the book, which includes URLs to the referenced site.

Conventions in This Book

When the text mentions "class" and "instance" in a general sense, they refer to a class that has a descriptor attribute and to instances of such classes, respectively. All other classes and instances will be referred to more specifically.

New in the 2nd Edition

The 2nd edition is an update including new features of Python as well as new ideas to learn. One of the new things is incredibly important if this book wants to maintain the status of "comprehensive" guide that it strives for. This important addition is about the addition of __set_name__() to the descriptor protocol in Python 3.6. You can read about this in Chapter 7, "Storing the Attributes".

Another addition is an idea that was inspired by looking into the __set_name__() addition to the protocol, which you'll see just after the section on that addition. Also, I added a chapter on creating instance-level descriptors, which were added to descriptor-tools well before this edition really got started.

The next thing is actually a change, not an addition. Since writing the first book, I found out about the built-in function vars(). Calling vars(obj) is equivalent to obj.__dict__, but is more Pythonic. Kind of like calling len(obj) instead of obj.__len__(). So the code examples have been updated to use vars(). Any remaining references to __dict__ are purposeful.

Pretty much everything else new in this edition is just cleaning up the language to be more legible.

PART I

About Descriptors

Part I is a deep explanation of what descriptors are, how they work, and how they're used. It gives enough information that you should be able to look at any descriptor and understand how it works and why it works that way, assuming the writer of the code made the code legible enough.

Creating your own descriptors isn't difficult once you have the information from Part I, but little to no guidance is given to help with it. Instead, Part II covers that with a bunch of options for creating new descriptors, as well as tips for avoiding common mistakes.

CHAPTER 1

What Is a Descriptor?

Put very simply, a descriptor is a class that can be used to call a method with simple attribute access, but there's obviously more to it than that. It's difficult to explain beyond that without digging a little into how descriptors implemented. So, here's a high-level view of the descriptor protocol.

A descriptor implements at least one of these three methods: __get__(), __set__(), or __delete__(). Each of those methods has a list of parameters needed, which will be discussed a little later, and each is called by a different sort of access of the attribute the descriptor represents. Doing simple a.x access will call the __get__() method of x; setting the attribute using a.x = value will call the __set__() method of x; and using del a.x will call, as expected, the __delete__() method of x.

Note   Since version 3.6, there's another method that descriptors can take advantage of, called __set_name__(), but using just that method doesn't make it a descriptor the way any of the other three will. This method will be mostly ignored for a while, since it doesn't have as big a role into how descriptors work. It will only be mentioned where most relevant.

As stated, only one of the methods needs to be implemented in order to be considered a descriptor, but any number of them can be implemented. And, depending on descriptor type and on which methods

© Jacob Zimmerman 2018
J. Zimmerman, *Python Descriptors*, https://doi.org/10.1007/978-1-4842-3727-4_1

are implemented, not implementing certain methods can restrict certain types of attribute access or provide interesting alternative behaviors for them. There are two types of descriptors based on which sets of these methods are implemented: data and non-data.

Data Descriptors versus Non-Data Descriptors

A data descriptor implements at least __set__() or __delete__(), but can include both. Data descriptors also often include __get__() since it's rare to want to set something without also being able to get it too. You *can* get the value, even if the descriptor doesn't include __get__(), but it's either roundabout or the descriptor writes it to the instance. That will be discussed more later.

A non-data descriptor *only* implements __get__(). If it adds a __set__() or __delete__() method, it becomes a data descriptor.

Unfortunately, the PyPy interpreter (up to version 2.4.0) gets this a little bit wrong. It doesn't take __delete__() into consideration until it knows that it's a data descriptor, and PyPy doesn't believe something is a data descriptor unless __set__() is implemented. Luckily, since a huge majority of data descriptors implement __set__(), this rarely becomes a problem.

It may seem like the distinction is pointless, but it is not. It comes into play upon attribute lookup. This will be discussed more later, but basically, the distinction is the types of uses it provides.

The Use of Descriptors by Python

It is worth noting that descriptors are an inherent part of how Python works. Python is known to be a multi-paradigm language, and as such supports paradigms such as functional programming, imperative programming, and object-oriented programming. This book does not attempt to go into depth about the different paradigms; only the object-oriented programming paradigm will be observed. Descriptors are used implicitly in Python for the language's object-oriented mechanisms. As will be explained shortly, methods are implemented using descriptors. As you may guess from reading this, it is thanks to descriptors that object-oriented programming is possible in Python. Descriptors are very powerful and advanced, and this book aims to teach Python programmers how to use them fully.

Summary

As you have seen, descriptors occupy a large part of the Python language, as they can replace attribute access with method calls, and even restrict which types of attribute access is allowed. Now that you have a broad idea of how descriptors are implemented as well as their use by the language, we will dig a little deeper yet, gaining a better understanding of how they work.

CHAPTER 2

The Descriptor Protocol

In order to get a better idea of what descriptors are good for, let's finish showing the full descriptor protocol. It's time to see the full signatures of the protocol's methods and what the parameters are.

The __get__(self, instance, owner) Method

This method is clearly the method for retrieving whatever data or object the descriptor is meant to maintain. Obviously, self is a parameter, since it's a method. Also, it receives instance and/or owner. We'll start with owner.

owner is the class that the descriptor is accessed from, or else the class of the instance it's being accessed from. When you make the call A.x (**A** being a class), and x is a descriptor object with __get__(), it's called with an owner with the instance set to None. So the lookup gets effectively transformed into A.__dict__['x'].__get__(None, A). This lets the descriptor know that __get__() is being called from a class, not an instance. owner is also often written to have a default value of None, but that's largely an optimization that only built-in descriptors take advantage of.

Now, onto the last parameters. instance is the instance that the descriptor is being accessed from, if it is being accessed from an instance. As previously stated, if None is passed into instance, the descriptor knows

© Jacob Zimmerman 2018
J. Zimmerman, *Python Descriptors*, https://doi.org/10.1007/978-1-4842-3727-4_2

that it's being called from the class level. But, if instance is *not* None, then it tells the descriptor which instance it's being called from. So an a.x call will be effectively translated to type(a).__dict__['x'].__get__(a, type(a)). Notice that it still receives the instance's class. Notice also that the call still starts with type(a), not just **a**, because descriptors are stored on classes. In order to be able to apply per-instance as well as per-class functionality, descriptors are given instance *and* owner (the class of the instance). How this translation and application happens will be discussed later.

Remember—and this applies to __set__() and __delete__() as well—self is an instance of the descriptor itself. It is not the instance that the descriptor is being called from; the instance parameter is the instance the descriptor is being called from. This may sound confusing at first, but don't worry if you don't understand for now—everything will be explained further.

The __get__() method is the only one that bothers to get the class separately. That's because it's the only method on non-data descriptors, which are generally made at a class level. The built-in decorator classmethod is implemented using descriptors and the __get__() method. In that case, it will use the owner parameter alone.

The __set__(self, instance, value) Method

As mentioned, __set__() does not have an owner parameter that accepts a class. __set__() does not need it, since data descriptors are generally designed for storing per-instance data. Even if the data is being stored on a per-class level, it should be stored internally without needing to reference the class.

self should be self-explanatory now; the next parameter is instance. This is the same as it is in the __get__() method. In this case, though, your initial call is a.x = someValue, which is then translated into type(a).__dict__['x'].__set__(a, someValue).

The last parameter is value, which is the value the attribute is being assigned.

One thing to note: when setting an attribute that is currently a descriptor from the class level, it will replace the descriptor with whatever is being set. For example, A.x = someValue does not get translated to anything; someValue replaces the descriptor object stored in x. To act on the class, see the following note.

The __delete__(self, instance) Method

After having learned about the __get__() and __set__() methods, __delete__() should be easy to figure out. self and instance are the same as in the other methods, but this method is invoked when del a.x is called and is translated to type(a).__dict__['x'].__delete__(a).

Do not accidentally name it __del__(), as that won't work as intended. __del__() would be the destructor of the descriptor instance, not of the attribute stored within.

It must be noted that, again, that __delete__() does not work from the class level, just like __set__(). Using del from the class level will remove the descriptor from the class' dictionary rather than calling the descriptor's __delete__() method.

Note   If you want a descriptor's __set__() or __delete__() methods to work from the class level, that means that the descriptor must be created on the class' metaclass. When doing so, everything that refers to owner is referring to the metaclass, while a reference to instance refers to the class. After all, classes are just instances of metaclasses. The section on metadescriptors will explain that in greater detail.

Summary

That's the sum total of the descriptor protocol. Having a basic idea of how it works, you'll now get a high-level view of the types of things that can be done with descriptors.

CHAPTER 3

What Are Descriptors Good For?

Nothing is perfect in this world, and Python's descriptors are no exception. Descriptors allow you to do some pretty cool things, but those cool things come at a cost. Here, we discuss the good and the bad.

Pros of Python Descriptors

Obviously we're going to go over the good things about descriptors. Would there be an entire book about them if they couldn't be considered a good thing?

Encapsulation

One of the most useful aspects of descriptors is that they encapsulate data so well. With descriptors, you can access an attribute the simple way using attribute access notation (`a.x`) while having more complex actions happen in the background. For example, a `Circle` class might have radius, diameter, circumference, and area all available as if they were attributes, but since they're all linked, you only need to store one (we'll use the radius for the example) and calculate the others based on it. But from the outside, they all look like attributes stored on the object.

© Jacob Zimmerman 2018
J. Zimmerman, *Python Descriptors*, https://doi.org/10.1007/978-1-4842-3727-4_3

Reuse of Read/Write Patterns

Using specialized descriptors, you can reuse code that you used with reading and/or writing of attributes. These can be used for repetitious attributes within the same class or attribute types shared by other classes as well. Some examples of reusable patterns are described in the following sections.

Lazy Instantiation

You can use descriptors to define a really simple syntax for lazily instantiating an attribute. There will be code provided for a nice lazy attribute implementation later in the book.

In the Circle example, the non-radius attributes, after having their caches invalidated, don't need to calculate their values right away; they could wait until they're needed. That's laziness.

Validation

Many descriptors are written simply to make sure that data being passed in conforms to the class' or attribute's invariants. Such descriptors can usually be designed as handy decorators, too.

Again with the Circle example: all of those attributes should be positive, so all the descriptors could also make sure the value being set is positive.

Triggering Actions

Descriptors can be used to trigger certain actions when the attribute is accessed. For example, the observer pattern can be implemented in a per-attribute sense to trigger calls to the observer whenever an attribute is changed.

Last `Circle` example: all the "attributes" are based on the radius calculated lazily. In order to keep from having to calculate them every time, you could cache the result. Then, whenever one of them changes, it could trigger invalidating all the others' caches.

Writing for the Class Level

Because descriptors are stored at the class scope instead of the instance scope, it allows you to do more robust things at the class level. For instance, descriptors make `classmethod` and `staticmethod` work, which will be explained in the next chapter.

Cons of Python Descriptors

As great as descriptors are, they come at a cost, just like just about everything else in programming.

Encapsulation

Wait... encapsulation was a pro. How can it also be a con? The problem is that you can hide incredible amounts of complexity behind something that just looks like attribute use. With getters and setters, the user at least sees that there's a function being called, and plenty can happen in a single function call. But the user won't necessarily expect that what is seemingly attribute access is causing something else to happen, too. Most of the time, this isn't a problem, but it can get in the user's way of trying to debug any problems, since *clearly* that code can't be a problem.

Can Be Difficult To Write

It can be easy for the mind to get all twisted up when it comes to thinking about the fact that descriptors are stored at the class level, but are usually for dealing with attributes at the instance level. Besides that, there are a lot of considerations and common pitfalls to deal with when deciding how to save the represented attribute, whether you decide to do it on the descriptor or on the the object that the attribute is for. The descriptor-tools library was created specifically because of this.

Additional Objects

Because descriptors add another layer of indirection/abstraction to the mix, they also add at least one additional object in memory, along with at least one additional call stack level. In most cases, it'll be more than one of each. This adds bloat that could at least be partially mitigated using getters and setters.

Summary

Descriptors are awesome, allowing for a variety of nice features that are good at hiding their complexity from users of your code, but you should definitely be aware that the power comes with cost.

CHAPTER 4

Descriptors in the Standard Library

There are three basic, well-known descriptors that come with Python: `property`, `classmethod`, and `staticmethod`. There's also a fourth one that you use all the time, but are less likely to know is a descriptor.

Of all the descriptors being shown in this chapter, it's possible that you only knew of `property` as a descriptor. Plenty of people even learn the basics of descriptors from it, but a lot of people don't know that `classmethod` and `staticmethod` are descriptors. They feel like super magical constructs built into the language that no one could reproduce in pure Python. Once someone has an understanding of descriptors, though, their basic implementation becomes relatively obvious. In fact, example code will be provided for all three in simplified, pure Python code.

Lastly, it will be shown that *all* methods are actually implemented with descriptors. Normal methods are actually done "magically," since the descriptor creation is implicit, but it's still not entirely magical because it's done using a language construct the anyone could create.

What I find really interesting is that the first three are all function decorators, which are another really awesome feature of Python that deserves its own book, even though they're way simpler.

© Jacob Zimmerman 2018
J. Zimmerman, *Python Descriptors*, https://doi.org/10.1007/978-1-4842-3727-4_4

The property Class

This book doesn't include instructions for how to use the property class and decorator; it is focused on understanding and creating descriptors. The official documentation for using property can be found in Python's documentation[2].

Of all the descriptors out there, property is likely the most versatile. This is because it doesn't really do anything on its own, but rather allows the users to inject their wanted functionality into it by providing their own getters, setters, and deleters.

To get a better idea of how it works, here is a simplified pure Python implementation of property.

```python
class property:
    def __init__(self, fget=None, fset=None, fdel=None):
        self.fget = fget
        self.fset = fset
        self.fdel = fdel

    def __get__(self, instance, owner):
        if instance is None:
            return self
        elif self.fget is None:
            raise AttributeError("unreadable attribute")
        else:
            return self.fget(instance)

    def __set__(self, instance, value):
        if self.fset is None:
            raise AttributeError("can't set attribute")
        else:
            self.fset(instance, value)
```

```python
def __delete__(self, instance):
    if self.fdel is None:
        raise AttributeError("can't delete attribute")
    else:
        self.fdel(instance)

def getter(self, fget):
    return type(self)(fget, self.fset, self.fdel)

def setter(self, fset):
    return type(self)(self.fget, fset, self.fdel)

def deleter(self, fdel):
    return type(self)(self.fget, self.fset, fdel)
```

As you can now see, the property class has almost no real functionality of its own; it simply delegates to the functions given to it. When a function is not provided for a certain method to delegate to, property assumes that it is a forbidden action and raises an AttributeError with an appropriate message.

A nice thing about the property class is that it largely just accepts methods. Even its constructor, which can be given all three methods at once, is capable of being called with just one, or even none. Because of this, the constructor and other methods can be used as decorators in a very convenient syntax. Check out the documentation[2] to learn more about it.

Omitted from this code example is the doc functionality, where it sets its own __doc__ property based on what is passed in through __init__()'s doc parameter or using __doc__ from fget if nothing is given. Also omitted is the code that sets other attributes on property, such as __name__, in order to help it appear even more like a simple attribute. They did not seem important enough to worry about, since the focus was more on the main functionality.

The classmethod Descriptor

classmethod is another descriptor that can be used as a decorator, but, unlike property, there's no good reason *not* to use it as one. classmethod is an interesting concept that doesn't exist in many other languages (if any). Python's type system, which uses classes as objects, makes classmethods easy and worthwhile to make.

Here's the Python code for classmethod.

```
class classmethod:
    def __init__(self, func):
        self.func = func

    def __get__(self, instance, owner):
        return functools.partial(self.func, owner)
```

That's all there is to it. classmethod is a non-data descriptor, so it only implements __get__(). This __get__() method completely ignores the instance parameter because, as "class" in the name implies, the method has nothing to do with an instance of the class and only deals with the class itself. What's really nice is the fact that this can still be called from an instance without any issues.

Why does the __get__() method return a functools.partial object with the owner passed in, though? To understand this, think about the parameter list of a function marked as a classmethod. The first parameter is the class parameter, usually named cls. This class parameter is filled in the call to partial so that the returned function can be called with just the arguments the user wants to explicitly provide. The true implementation doesn't use partial, but works similarly.

Again, the code that sets __name__, __doc__, etc. is omitted to show only how the main functionality works.

The staticmethod Descriptor

A method marked with staticmethod is strange in that it's a method that is really just a function, but it is "attached" to a class. Being part of the class doesn't do anything other than show users that it is associated with that class and giving it a more specific namespace. Also, interestingly, because staticmethod and classmethod are implemented using descriptors, they're inherited by subclasses.

The implementation of staticmethod is even simpler than that of classmethod; it just accepts a function and then returns it when __get__() is called.

```
class staticmethod:
    def __init__(self, func):
        self.func = func

    def __get__(self, instance, owner):
        return self.func
```

Regular Methods

Remember that it was stated earlier that regular methods implicitly use descriptors as well. In fact, all functions can be used as methods. This is because functions are non-data descriptors as well as callables.

Here is a Python implementation that roughly shows how a function looks.

```
class function:
    def __call__(self, *args, **kwargs):
        # do something
```

```
def __get__(self, instance, owner=None):
    if instance is None:
        return self
    else:
        return functools.partial(self, instance)
```

This is not a very accurate representation; the return statements are a bit off. When you access a method from an instance without calling it, the returned object isn't a partial object; it is a "bound method". A "bound method" is one that has self already "bound" to it, but has yet to be called, passing in the other arguments if needed. When it's called from the class, it only returns the function itself. In Python 2, this was an "unbound method," which is basically the same thing. This idea of creating "unbound" versions when instance is None comes up later, so keep it in mind.

Summary

In this chapter, we've seen the most common built-in descriptors. Now that we've seen some examples, let's get a closer, better look at how they work by digging into the real differences between data and non-data descriptors.

CHAPTER 5

Attribute Access and Descriptors

It was stated earlier that attribute access calls are transformed into descriptor calls, but it was not stated how. The quick answer is that __getattribute__(), __setattr__(), and __delattr__() do it. That probably isn't much of an answer for you, so I'll dig into it more. These three methods exist on all normal objects, inherited via the object class (and classes inherit it from the type metaclass). As you might imagine, these methods are called when an attribute on an object is retrieved, set, or deleted, respectively, and it is these methods that decide whether to use a descriptor, __dict__, or __slots__, and whether to return/set something on the class or on the instance.

An explanation of this decision process is given in a little bit, but now I have to explain something that may be nagging you: Why do the set and and delete methods end with attr, but the get method ends with attribute?

Part of the answer to that is the fact that there actually *is* a __getattr__() method, but it's not used quite the same as the others. __getattribute__() handles all the normal attribute lookup logic while __getattr__() is called by __getattribute__() in a last ditch effort if all else fails. It is recommended by Python that you don't make changes to __getattribute__() except under extreme circumstances, and only if you really know what you're doing. With some experience, I can concur with that recommendation.

© Jacob Zimmerman 2018
J. Zimmerman, *Python Descriptors*, https://doi.org/10.1007/978-1-4842-3727-4_5

I don't know why setting and deleting don't have a similar setup, but I can theorize. It might have to do with the idea that a typical override of attribute lookup *is* as a failsafe if the usual ways don't work, but if someone is overriding one or both of the others, there's a decent chance that it may be a complete replacement or at least the first thing tried instead of the backup thing. Plus, there's the fact that, under normal circumstances (doesn't use __slots__, isn't a named tuple, etc.), setting always works and deleting is pretty rare. But you may want to ask one of the core developers if you're really that curious.

One last clarification: near the beginning of the book, I said that attribute access gets "transformed" into calls to the descriptor methods. This makes it sound like it's a compile-time decision, but it's not. Python is a dynamically typed language, and it isn't supposed to know at compile time whether an attribute exists on an object and whether it needs to be accessed like a descriptor or just a normal attribute, especially since this can change at runtime. It can make certain guesses based on the code around it, but it can never be 100% sure.

No, using attributes *effectively* gets transformed into calls to the descriptor method within the methods mentioned previously, which describe how the language decides what to do. This is the really dynamic part. So let's move on and see what this decision-making process look like.

Instance Access

Simply looking up attributes is the most complex of the three uses of attributes because there are multiple places to look for attributes: on the instance and on the class. Also, if it's a descriptor on the class, you have two different behaviors for data and non-data descriptors.

__getattribute__() has an order of priority that describes where to look for attributes and how to deal with them. That priority is the main difference between data descriptors and non-data descriptors. Here is that list of priorities:

- Data descriptors

- Instance attributes

- Non-data descriptors and class attributes

- __getattr__ (might be called separately from __getattribute__)

The first thing __getattribute__() does is look in the class dictionary for the attribute. If it's not found, it works its way through the method resolution order (MRO) of classes (the superclasses in a linear order) to continue looking for it. If it's still not found, it'll move to the next priority. If it *is* found, it is checked to see if it is a data descriptor. If it's not, it moves on to the next priority. If it turns out to be a data descriptor, it'll call __get__() and return the result, assuming it has a __get__() method. If it doesn't have a __get__() method, then it moves on to the next priority.

That's a lot of ifs, and that's just within the first priority to determine whether a viable data descriptor is available to work with. Luckily, the next priority is simpler.

Next in the priority list is checking the instance dictionary (or slots, if that's what the object is using). If it exists there, we simply return that. Otherwise, it moves to the next priority.

In this priority, it checks through the class dictionaries again, working its way down the MRO list if needed. If nothing is found, it moves to the next priority. Otherwise, it checks the found object to see if it's a descriptor (at this point, we only need to check if it's a non-data descriptor because if we've made it this far, it's definitely not a data descriptor). If so, it calls the descriptor's __get__() method and returns the result. Otherwise, it simply returns the object. This time, it doesn't have a backup of returning the descriptor object itself if it doesn't have __get__() because it, being a non-data descriptor, guarantees that it has __get__().

If all else has failed up to this point, it checks with __getattr__() for any possible custom behavior regarding attribute access. If there's nothing, an AttributeError is raised.

With this complicated definition, Python users should be grateful that a lot of work has been put into optimizing this access algorithm to the point that it's remarkably fast. The flowchart in Figure 5-1 show how descriptors are accessed, with blue bands denoting each priority.

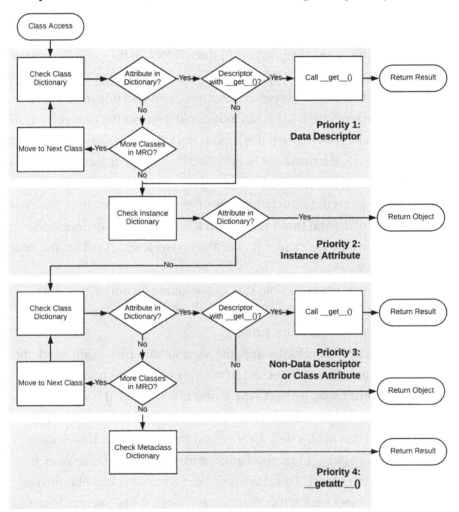

Figure 5-1. *Class access*

In the common case where the class' metaclass is type, or there are no new attributes on the metaclass, class access can be viewed in a simplified way compared to instance access; it doesn't even have a priority list. It still uses __getattribute__(), but it's the one defined on its metaclass. It simply searches through the class dictionaries, progressing through the MRO as needed. If found, it checks to see if it's a descriptor with the __get__() method. If so, it makes the proper call and returns the result. Otherwise, it just returns the object. At the class level, though, it doesn't care if the descriptor is data or non-data; if the descriptor has a __get__() method, the method is used.

If nothing was found, an AttributeError is raised, as shown in Figure 5-2.

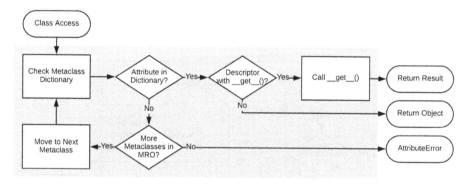

Figure 5-2. *An AttributeError is raised*

Unfortunately, if there *are* new attributes on the metaclass, this simplification is unhelpful, since they might be used in the lookup. In fact, class access looks almost exactly like instance access (replacing "class" with "metaclass" and "instance" with "class") with one big difference. Instead of checking just the current instance/class dictionary, it checks through the MRO of it as well. It also still treats descriptors on the class as descriptors, rather than automatically returning the descriptor object. Knowing this, Figure 5-3 shows the *full* class access diagram, with all the priority levels.

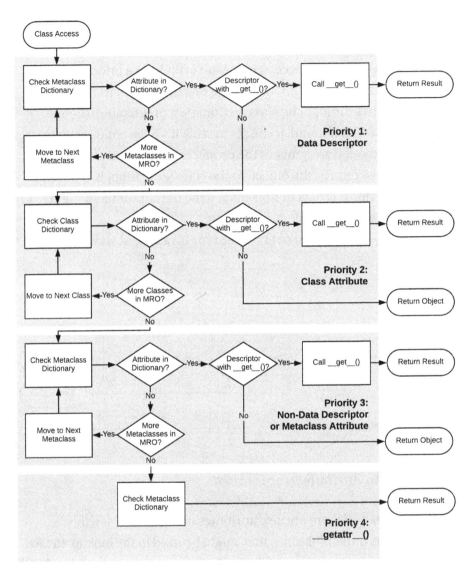

Figure 5-3. *The full class access diagram*

Set and Delete Calls

Setting and deleting are just a little bit different. If the required __set__()
or __delete__() method doesn't exist, and it's a data descriptor, an
AttributeError is raised. The other difference is the fact that setting
and deleting never get beyond the instance priority. If the attribute
doesn't exist on the instance, setting will add it and deleting will raise an
AttributeError.

Figure 5-4 shows the last flowchart, depicting what happens for setting
and deleting.

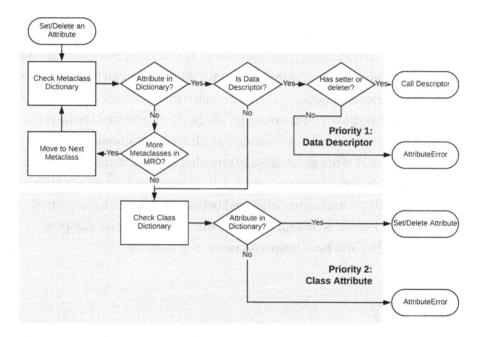

Figure 5-4. *The setting and deleting processes*

The Reasoning Behind Data versus Non-Data Descriptors

Now that the difference between data and non-data descriptors has been explained, it should be explained *why* these two versions exist.

The first place to look at is the built-in use cases for each type within the language and standard library. The prime example of a data descriptor is `property`. As its name suggests, its purpose is to create properties for classes (replace getter and setter methods with a syntax that looks like simple attribute use). That means class-level access is not intended since properties represent fields on an instance.

Meanwhile, the primary use-case for non-data descriptors is decorating methods for different usages (`classmethod`, `staticmethod`, and especially the implicit descriptor used for normal methods). While these can be called from instances (and normal methods *should* be called from instances), they're not meant to be *set* or *deleted* from instances. Methods are assigned on the class. A function can be assigned to an instance attribute, but it doesn't make it a method, since `self` is not automatically provided as the first argument when called. Also, when it comes to the "magic" dunder methods (methods with two leading and two trailing underscores) being called through the normal, "magical" way, Python is optimized to look directly on the class, skipping over anything that may have been assigned to the instance.

Summary

Rarely is it useful to know the *full* depth of what is happening behind the scenes of attribute calls, and even knowing the basic priority list rarely comes into play, since descriptors generally do what is obvious, once you understand how they're accessed. There are times, though, when the priority list, and possibly even the full depth, will help in understanding why a descriptor isn't working as hoped or how to set up a descriptor to do a more complicated task.

PART II

Making Descriptors

Finally, the fun part has arrived. Despite the simplicity of the descriptor protocol, there are so many ways that a descriptor can be used and made that, even though that last part was pretty long, this section is going to be much longer.

Part I tells you enough for you to go and make your own descriptors, but it doesn't give any tips, patterns, or real guidance for doing so. Part II is filled to the brim with those.

CHAPTER 6

Which Methods Are Needed?

When designing a descriptor, it must be decided which methods will be included. It can sometimes help to decide right away if the descriptor should be a data or non-data descriptor, but sometimes it works better to "discover" which kind of descriptor it is.

__delete__() is rarely ever needed, even if it is a data descriptor. That doesn't mean it shouldn't ever be included, however. If the descriptor is going to be released into an open domain, it wouldn't hurt to add the __delete__() method on a data descriptor simply for completeness for cases when a user decides to call del on it. If you don't, an AttributeError will be raised when someone tries to delete it.

__get__() is almost always needed for data *and* non-data descriptors. It is required for non-data descriptors, and the typical case where __get__() isn't required for data descriptors is if __set__() assigns the data into the instance dictionary under the same name as the descriptor (what I call set-it-and-forget-it descriptors). Otherwise, it is almost always wanted for retrieving the data that is set in a data descriptor, so unless the data is assigned to the instance to be automatically retrieved without __get__() or the data is write-only, a __get__() method would be necessary. Keep in mind that if a descriptor doesn't have a __get__() method and instance doesn't have anything in __dict__ under the same name as the descriptor, the actual descriptor object itself will be returned.

© Jacob Zimmerman 2018
J. Zimmerman, *Python Descriptors*, https://doi.org/10.1007/978-1-4842-3727-4_6

Just like __delete__(), __set__() is only used for data descriptors. Unlike __delete__(), __set__() is not regarded as unnecessary. Seeing that __delete__() is unused in the most common cases, __set__() is nearly a requirement for creating data descriptors (which need either __set__() or __delete__()). If the descriptor's status as data or non-data is being "discovered," __set__() is usually the deciding factor. Even if the data is meant to be read-only, __set__() should be included to raise an AttributeError in order to enforce the read-only nature. Otherwise, it may just be treated like non-data descriptor.

When __get__() Is Called Without an instance Argument

It is often that a descriptor's __get__() method is the most complicated method on it because there are two different ways it can be called: with or without an instance argument (although "without" means that None is given instead of an instance).

When the descriptor is a class-level descriptor (usually non-data), implementing __get__() without using instance is trivial, since that's the intended use. But when a descriptor is meant for instance-level use, and the descriptor is not being called from an instance, it can be difficult to figure out what to do.

Here, I present a few options.

Raise Exception or Return self

The first thing that may come to mind is to raise an exception, since class-level access is not intended, but this should be avoided. A common programming style in Python is called *EAFP*, meaning that it is *easier to ask for forgiveness than for permission*. What this means is that, just because something isn't used as intended, it doesn't mean that usage should be disallowed. If the use will hurt invariants and cause problems, it's fine to disallow it by raising an exception; otherwise, there are other, better options to consider. The conventional solution is to simply return self. If the descriptor is being accessed from the class level, it's likely that the user realizes that it's a descriptor and wants to work with it. Doing so can be a sign of inappropriate use, but Python allows freedom, and so should its users, to a point. The property built-in will return self (the property object) if accessed from the class, as an example. From what I've seen, this is the most common approach by far.

"Unbound" Attributes

Another solution, which is used by methods, is to have an "unbound" version of the attribute be returned. When accessing a function from the class level, the function's __get__() detects that it does not have an instance, and so just returns the function itself. In Python 2, it actually returned an "unbound" method, which is where the name I use comes from. In Python 3, though, they changed it to just the function, since that's exactly what it is anyway.

This can work for non-callable attributes as well. It's a little strange, since it turns the attribute into a callable that must receive an instance to return the value. This makes it into a specific attribute lookup, akin to len() and iter(), where you just need to pass in the instance to receive the wanted value.

Here is a stripped-down __get__() implementation that works this way.

```
def __get__(self, instance, owner):
    if instance is None:
        def unboundattr(inst):
            return self.__get__(inst, owner)
        return unboundattr
    else:
        ...
```

When called, the inner unboundattr() function will end up using the else branch of the __get__() method (assuming they didn't pass in None). Using inner functions can sometimes be confusing, and typing that whole thing every time is a little annoying, so here's a reusable class implementation that can be used by any descriptor.

```
class UnboundAttribute:
    def __init__(self, descriptor, owner):
        self.descriptor = descriptor
        self.owner = owner

    def __call__(self, instance):
        return self.descriptor.__get__(instance, self.owner)
```

Using this class, a __get__() method that uses unbound attributes can be implemented like this:

```
def __get__(self, instance, owner):
    if instance is None:
        return UnboundAttribute(self, owner)
    else:
        ...
```

The original version relies on closures around self and owner, which remove its reusability, other than through copying and pasting. But the class takes those two variables in with its constructor to store on a new instance. It's also kind of nice that if you print the unbound attribute object, it says that it's an unbound attribute. (This also works if you implement your own version, especially if you take in some handy metadata, like the name of the attribute being accessed. More on how to do that in the next chapter.)

The really interesting (and useful) thing about this technique is that the unbound attribute can be passed into a higher-order function that receives a function, such as map( ). It avoids having to write up a getter method or ugly lambda. For example, if there was a class like this:

```
class Class:
    attr = UnbindableDescriptor()
```

A map( ) call to a list of Class objects like this:

```
result = map(lambda c: c.attr, aList)
```

could be replaced with this:

```
result = map(Class.attr, aList)
```

Instead of passing in a lambda to do the work of accessing the attribute of the Class instances, Class.attr is passed in, which returns the "unbound" version of the attribute—a function that receives the instance in order to look up the attribute on the descriptor. In essence, the descriptor provides an implicit getter method to the reference of the attribute.

This is a very useful technique for implementing a descriptor's __get__( ) method, but it has one major drawback: returning self is so prevalent that not doing so is highly unexpected. Hopefully, this idea gets some traction in the community and becomes the new standard. Also, as seen in the upcoming chapter on read-only descriptors, there may need to be a way to access the descriptor object. Luckily, all you need to do is get the descriptor attribute from the returned UnboundAttribute.

Even though it's not the expected behavior, the built-in function descriptor already does this, so it won't be too difficult for them to get used to it. People expect "unbound method" functions when accessing from the class level, so applying the convention to attributes shouldn't be a huge stretch for them.

Since writing the first edition of this book, I have discovered that there is a function for creating unbound attributes in the standard library, and it's more useful than UnboundAttribute in some important ways. In the operator module, there's a function called attrgetter() that takes in a string name of an attribute and returns a function that takes in an instance and (I assume) calls getattr() on the instance with the name of the attribute. There's also support for multiple attribute names being passed in; the final result is a tuple of all those attributes on the instance.

There are several significant benefits to this over descriptor-based unbound attributes (without even counting the multiple attribute support). The first is greater support for inheritance. If a subclass overrode the descriptor with a different one, but the superclass version is passed around, it will actually use the superclass descriptor, which removes the awesome dynamic nature of inheritance. For this very same reason, unless you're absolutely sure that the class you're using doesn't have any subclasses, you should use attrgetter() for methods as well.

Descriptor-based unbound attributes can support the same level of inheritance support, but there's more work involved. First, you need the name of the attribute, which isn't always easy to get. Again, methods for doing so are in the next chapter. After that, the changes are pretty simple. You change __call__() to use getattr() instead of descriptor.__get__(). This then eliminates the need for the descriptor and owner properties, though you should keep descriptor so someone can look up the descriptor, as mentioned earlier. Sadly, I don't see any practical way of supporting multiple attributes this way.

The second major benefit is that it works for all kinds of attributes, not just methods or descriptor-based ones.

There are a few downsides to attrgetter() though. First, and maybe most obvious, is the lack of code completion help. You're passing in the string name of an attribute, which means whatever editor you're using is not going to help you not screw up the spelling of the attribute's name. Second, it loses a little bit of context. When a class name is used, you include the context that attribute name applies to, whereas attrgetter() only includes the name of the attribute.

If you do the upgrades to `UnboundAttribute`, I still completely support using it. But it is certainly good to know when to use `attrgetter()` instead.

Summary

We've looked into the decision-making process behind building general descriptors and figuring out which methods we'll want and possibly using unbound attributes with `__get__()`. In the next chapter, we'll dig into even more design decisions that have to be made, at least when it comes to storing values with descriptors.

CHAPTER 7

Storing the Attributes

Now that all the preliminaries are out of the way, it is time to see the part of descriptors that is useful: storing the attributes that the descriptor represents. There are a lot of ways to store attributes with a descriptor, and this chapter will go over every option that I'm aware of, starting with the easiest.

Class-Level Storage

Class-level storage is easy; it's normal storage on the descriptor. As an example, here is a descriptor that creates a basic class-level variable:

```
class ClassAttr:
    def __init__(self, value):
        self.value = value

    def __get__(self, instance, owner):
        return self.value

    def __set__(self, instance, value):
        self.value = value
```

This descriptor saves a value on itself as a typical instance attribute, which is simply returned in the __get__() method, ignoring whether instance is provided or not, since it's a class-level attribute. This attribute can also be accessed through an instance, but making any change to it from the instance will apply the change to every instance of the class.

© Jacob Zimmerman 2018
J. Zimmerman, *Python Descriptors*, https://doi.org/10.1007/978-1-4842-3727-4_7

Unfortunately, due to __set__() not being called when a descriptor is accessed from the class level, the variable storing the descriptor will be reassigned to the new value, rather than it being passed to __set__().

For more details about making class-level descriptors that __set__() and __delete__() can be used on, check out the section at the end of this chapter about metadescriptors.

Descriptors aren't just for class-level attributes, though; they're used for instance-level attributes too. There are two broad strategies for storing instance-level attributes with descriptors:

- On the descriptor

- In the instance dictionary

Each strategy has some hurdles to clear for a reusable descriptor. When storing it on the descriptor, there are hurdles as to how to store it without memory leaks or hashing issues. As for storing the attributes on the instance dictionary, the difficulty comes from trying to figure out what name to store it under in the dictionary to avoid clashing.

Storing Data on the Descriptor

As shown before, saving a simple value on the descriptor is how a class-level value is stored. What must be done to store a value on a per-instance basis in one place? What is needed is some way to map an instance to its attribute value. Well, another name for a mapping is a dictionary. Maybe a dictionary would work. Here's what using a dictionary for its storage might look like.

```
class Descriptor:
    def __init__(self):
        self.storage = {}

    def __get__(self, instance, owner):
        return self.storage[instance]
```

```
def __set__(self, instance, value):
    self.storage[instance] = value

def __delete__(self, instance):
    del self.storage[instance]
```

The __get__() method doesn't deal with the if instance is None case, and in all other examples, it will be ignored for the sake of brevity and removing distractions while reading the code.

The dict in the code example has solved our first issue of storage per instance. Unfortunately, there are a couple shortcomings to using a plain old dict for the job.

The first shortcoming to address is memory leaks. A typical dict will store the instance used as the key long after the object should have been otherwise garbage collected from lack of use. This is fine for short-lived programs that won't use a lot of memory and if the instances don't suffer from the second shortcoming mentioned later, but if this isn't the case, we need a way to deal with the issue.

Let's look at how to get around this problem. The descriptor needs a way to stop caring about instances that are no longer in use. The weakref module provides just that. Weak references allow variables to reference an instance as long as there is a normal reference to it somewhere, but allow it to be garbage collected otherwise. They also allow you to specify behavior that will run as soon as the reference is removed.

The module also provides a few collections that are designed to remove items from themselves as the items are garbage collected. Of those, we want to look at a WeakKeyDictionary. A WeakKeyDictionary keeps a weak reference to its key, and therefore once the instance that is used as the key is no longer in use, the dictionary cleans the entire entry out.

So, here's the example again, this time using the WeakKeyDictionary.

```
from weakref import WeakKeyDictionary
class Descriptor:
    def __init__(self):
        self.storage = WeakKeyDictionary()

    def __get__(self, instance, owner):
        return self.storage[instance]

    def __set__(self, instance, value):
        self.storage[instance] = value

    def __delete__(self, instance):
        del self.storage[instance]
```

Every change between the previous example and this one has been made bold, and this shows that there really isn't much of a difference. The only difference is that the special dictionary needs to be imported and a WeakKeyDictionary needs to be created instead of the normal dict. This is a very easy upgrade to make, and many descriptor guides stop here. It works in most situations, so it isn't a bad solution.

Unfortunately, it still suffers from the other shortcoming that a regular dict does: it doesn't support unhashable types.

To use an object as a key in a dict, it must be hashable. There are a few built-in types that cannot be hashed, namely the mutable collections (list, set, and dict), and maybe a few more. Any object that is mutable (values inside can be changed) and overrides __eq__() to compare internal values must be unhashable. If the object is changed in a way that changes equality, suddenly the hash code changes so that it can't be looked up as a dictionary key. Thus, such mutable objects are generally advised to mark themselves as unhashable using __hash__ = None. Overriding __eq__() will do this automatically; overriding __hash__ should therefore be done only if equality is constant.

If it weren't for Python providing default implementations of __eq__()
and __hash__() (equality is the same as identity—an object is equal
to itself, and nothing else), most objects wouldn't be hashable and thus
supported for descriptors using a hashing collection. Luckily, this means
that types *are* hashable by default, but there are still many unhashable
types out there.

Again, the WeakKeyDictionary is *not* a bad solution; it just doesn't
cover all possibilities. Much of the time, it is good enough, but it generally
advised not to use it for public libraries, at least not without good warnings
in the documentation. After all, the descriptor protocol provides ways to set
and delete attributes, so they should support instances of mutable classes.

There needs to be a solution that doesn't suffer from this problem, and
there is. The simplest solution is to use the instance's ID as the key instead
of the instance itself. Hooray! Now the dictionary doesn't hold onto unused
instances anymore, and it doesn't require the classes to be hashable.

Here's what that solution would look like.

```python
class Descriptor:
    def __init__(self):
        self.storage = {}

    def __get__(self, instance, owner):
        return self.storage[id(instance)]

    def __set__(self, instance, value):
        self.storage[id(instance)] = value

    def __delete__(self, instance):
        del self.storage[id(instance)]
```

The example switches back to a normal dict, so the changes
mentioned are based on the differences between this example and the
first one again, rather than comparing to the previous one. Every time the
storage is being accessed, it's being accessed by id(instance) instead of
just instance.

This seems like a pretty good solution, since it doesn't suffer from either of the problems of the previous two solutions. But it's not a good solution. It doesn't suffer from exactly the same problems of the previous solutions, but it still suffers from a memory leak. Yes, the dictionary no longer stores the instances, so those aren't being kept, but there's no mechanism to clear useless IDs from the dictionary. In fact, there's a chance (it's a tiny chance, but it exists) that a new instance of the class may be created with the same ID of an older, deleted instance, so the new instance has an attribute equal to the old one until it's changed. That's assuming it *can* be changed; what if the descriptor is designed to be read-only (more on that later)? Then the new instance is absolutely stuck with the old value.

So, this still doesn't solve the on-descriptor storage problem, but it's leading in the right direction. What is needed is a storage system that works like a dictionary, with instance as the key, but uses id(instance) instead of hash(instance) for storage. It also needs to clean itself out if an instance is no longer in use.

Since such a thing isn't built in; it will have to be custom-made. Here is that custom dictionary, designed specifically for this book.

```
import weakref

class DescriptorStorage:
    def __init__(self, **kwargs):
        self.storage = {}
        for k, v in kwargs.items():
            self.__setitem__(k, v)

    def __getitem__(self, item):
        return self.storage[id(item)]

    def __setitem__(self, key, value):
        self.storage[id(key)] = value
```

```
weakref.finalize(key, self.storage.__delitem__,
id(key))

def __delitem__(self, key):
    del self.storage[id(key)]
```

The real version obviously has more methods, such as __iter__, __len__, etc., but the main three uses for storage with a descriptor are implemented here. The rest of the implementation can be found in the descriptor-tools library.

This class is surprisingly simple. The basics of it is that there is a facade class that acts like a dictionary, delegating most functionality to an inner dictionary, but transforming the given keys to their IDs. The only real difference is that, in __setitem__(), this new class creates a finalize weak reference, which takes a reference, a function, and any arguments to send to that function when the reference is garbage collected. In this case, it removes the item (again, stored using id()) from the internal dictionary.

The keys to how this storage class works are using an ID as the key (which means the instances do not need to be hashable) and weak reference callbacks (which remove unused objects from the dictionary). In essence, this class is a WeakKeyDictionary that internally uses the ID of the given key as the actual key.

Storing the attribute in the descriptor safely takes a lot more consideration than most people ever actually put into it, but now there is a nice, catch-all solution for doing that. The first two solutions are imperfect, but not useless. If the use case for the descriptor allows for the use of either of those solutions, it wouldn't hurt to consider them. They are viable enough for many cases and are likely to be slightly more performant than the custom storage system provided here. For public libraries, though, either the custom dictionary or a on-instance solution from the following section should be considered.

Storing on the Instance Dictionary

It's often better to store the data on the instance instead of within the descriptor, provided that a worthwhile strategy for deriving the key can be found. This is because it doesn't require an additional object for storage; the instance's built-in storage dictionary is used. However, some classes will define __slots__, and, as such, will not have the storage dictionary to mess with. This limits the usefulness of on-instance strategies a little bit, but __slots__ is used rarely enough that it's barely worth considering.

If you want to make a descriptor safe with __slots__ while still defaulting to using the instance dictionary, you may want to create some sort of alternative that uses on-descriptor storage when a Boolean flag is set on creation. There are plenty of ways to implement that, whether using a factory that chooses a different descriptor if the flag is set or the class within has alternate paths based on the flag value. Another, simpler alternative is to document the name that the descriptor stores its values under so that users of the descriptor who want to use __slots__ can prepare a slot for it. This requires that the descriptor does direct instance attribute setting (either with dot notation or with getattr(), setattr(), and delattr()) rather than getting the instance dictionary first.

Another way to go about this (which doesn't require explicitly asking the user) is to check if the class has the storage dictionary; if it does, then simply use it, but if it doesn't, you can store it on the descriptor instance directly. Checking for the existence of __slots__ is unreliable as subclasses may not define __slots__ (while the base class does), so they will have both an instance dictionary and __slots__.

Storing the data on the instance using the instance dictionary is easy (although often verbose, since referencing the attribute as vars(a)['x'] is often needed instead of a.x in order to avoid recursively calling the descriptor), as the following example will show. It's a simple example with a location of where to store the data being hard-coded as "desc_store".

```
class InstanceStoringDescriptorBasic:
    name = "desc_store"

    def __get__(self, instance, owner):
        return vars(instance)[self.name]

    def __set__(self, instance, value):
        vars(instance)[self.name] = value

    def __delete__(self, instance):
        del vars(instance)[self.name]
```

As shown, it is pretty easy to store on the instance. Some of you may
not know about vars(), though, so I will explain. Calling vars() on an
object returns the instance dictionary. Many of you probably knew about
__dict__. The vars() function returns that same dictionary and is the
preferred (read "Pythonic") way of accessing it, though lesser known.
It is preferred largely because of the lack of double underscores. Like
nearly every other "magic" attribute with double underscores, there is a
clean way of using it. Hopefully, now you will inform all of your Python-
using buddies about this and it can become a much more widely known
function.

But why should the values be accessed via vars() and not simple dot
notation? There are actually plenty of situations where using dot notation
would work just fine. In fact, it works in most situations. The only times
there are problems is when the data descriptor has the same name that is
being used for storage in the dictionary or if the name being used is not
a legal Python identifier. Often, this case pops up because the descriptor
is purposely storing the attribute under its own name, which is almost
guaranteed to prevent name conflicts. But it's still possible that an outside
data descriptor has the same name as where the main descriptor is trying
to store its data. In order to avoid this, it is preferable to always directly
reference the instance's dictionary. Another good reason is that it makes it
more explicit and obvious where the data is being stored.

The next thing to be figured out is how the descriptor knows the name to store the attribute under. Hopefully it's obvious that hard-coding a location is a bad idea; it prevents multiple instances of that type of descriptor from being used on the same class since they will all be contending for the same name.

Asking for the Location

The simplest way to get a location name is to ask for it in the constructor. A descriptor like that would look something like this:

```
class GivenNameInstanceStoringDescriptor:
    def __init__(self, name):
        self.name = name

    def __get__(self, instance, owner):
        return instance.__dict__[self.name]

    def __set__(self, instance, value):
        instance.__dict__[self.name] = value

    def __delete__(self, instance):
        del instance.__dict__[self.name]
```

The only real difference between this one and the previous one is that it has an __init__() method that receives the preferred location name from the user instead of hard-coding it. In fact, the rest of the code is exactly the same.

Asking for the location to store the attribute value is easy when it comes to creating the descriptor, but is tedious for the user and can even be dangerous in the event that the location is required to have the same name as the descriptor, since the user can mess that up. Such is the case with set-it-and-forget-it descriptors, such as the following descriptor, which is a descriptor used for validating data using the function provided.

```
class Validated:
    def __init__(self, name, validator):
        self.name = name
        self.validator = validator

    def __set__(self, instance, value):
        if self.validator(value):
            instance.__dict__[self.name] = value
        else:
            raise ValueError("not a valid value for" +
            self.name)
```

In this Validated descriptor, __init__() asks for the location to store the real data. Since this is a set-it-and-forget-it descriptor that lets the instance handle retrieval instead of providing a __get__(), the location that the user provides must be the same as the descriptor's name on the class in order for the descriptor to work as intended. For example, if a class was accidentally written like this:

```
class A:
    validatedAttr = Validated('validatedAttribute',
    validatorFunc)
```

validatedAttr is all screwed up. To set it, the user writes a.validatedAttr = someValue, but retrieving it requires the user to write a.validatedAttribute. This may not seem all that bad since it can be fixed easily, but these are the types of bugs that can often be very difficult to figure out and can take a long time to notice. Also, why should the user be required to write in the location when it can be derived somehow?

Set-It-and-Forget-It Descriptors

Now set-it-and-forget-it descriptors can finally be explained. Of the three methods in the descriptor protocol, these descriptors generally only

49

implement __set__(), as seen in the example. That's not always the case, though. For example the following lazy initialization descriptor only uses __get__().

```
class lazy:
    def __init__(self, func):
        self.func = func

    def __get__(self, instance, owner):
        value = self.func(instance)
        instance.__dict__[func.__name__] = value
        return value
```

This lazy descriptor can also be used as a decorator over a function, which it replaces and uses to do the lazy initialization. In this case, and in the case of other set-it-and-forget-it descriptors, the descriptor sets the value directly onto the instance, using the same name the descriptor is referenced by. This allows the descriptor to either be a non-data descriptor that is never used more than once—as in the case of lazy—or to be a data descriptor that has no need to implement __get__(), which is the case with most set-it-and-forget-it descriptors. In many cases, set-it-and-forget-it descriptors can increase lookup speeds by just looking in the instance or even provide other optimizations, like the lazy descriptor.

Indirectly Asking for the Location

Something else can be noted about the lazy descriptor from the set-it-and-forget-it section, and that's how it was able to determine where to store the attribute; it pulled it from the function that it decorated.

This is a great way to indirectly ask for the name of the descriptor. Since the descriptor, initialized as a decorator, is provided with a function that the descriptor is replacing, it can use that function's name to look up that name for a place to store the information on instance.

Name Mangling

Using the name directly like that, though, can be dangerous for most non-data descriptors, since setting it directly to that location would override its own access (which `lazy` actually intended to have happen). When building a non-data descriptor that doesn't want to write over itself—although the chances are probably pretty slim for that situation to come up—it is best to do some "name mangling" when storing the data. To do so, just add an underscore or two to the beginning of the name. Using at least two leading underscores and at most one trailing underscore causes Python to add its own mangling to the name; using one leading underscore simply signals that the attribute is "private" to those using the object. There's an incredibly low chance that the name is already taken on the `instance`.

Next, what can be done if asking the user for the name is a bad idea and the descriptor isn't also a decorator? How does a descriptor determine its name then? There are several options, and the first one that will be discussed is how a descriptor can try to dig up its own name.

Fetching the Name

It would seem so simple to just look up what a descriptor's name is, but, like any object, a descriptor could be assigned to multiple variables with different names. No, a more roundabout way of discovering one's own name is required.

Note   Inspiration for this technique is attributed to "The Zipline Show" on YouTube, specifically their video about descriptors[3]. This technique shows up around 22 minutes in. They may have gotten the technique from the book they mention at the beginning of the video, but I took the idea from them, not the book.

The original version of this technique that I adapted a little used the following code.

```
def name_of(self, instance):
    for attr in type(instance).__dict__:
        if attr.startswith('__'): continue
        obj = type(instance).__dict__[attr]
        if obj is self:
            self.name = self.mangle(attr)
            break
```

This method is meant to be added to any descriptor in order to look up its name. If the descriptor's name attribute isn't set, the descriptor just runs this method to set it. On the second to last line, it sends the name to a name mangler—which just makes sure it starts with two underscores— instead of using the name as it is. As mentioned in the name mangling section, this may be necessary, but not always.

There's a problem with this method, though: it doesn't handle subclasses. If a class with this descriptor is subclassed and an instance of that subclass tries to use the descriptor before an instance of the original class does, it will fail to look up its name. This is because the descriptor is on the original class, not the subclass, but the name_of() method looks in the class' dictionary for itself. The subclass will not have the descriptor in its dictionary.

Not to worry, though. The version in the library solves this problem by using dir() to get all the names of attributes, including from superclasses, and then it delegates those to a function that digs into the __dict__ of each class on the MRO until it finds what it's looking for. I also removed the name mangling function, allowing you to use that only as necessary. Lastly, it doesn't bother with ignoring attributes that start with a double underscore. Such a check may actually be slower than accessing the attribute and comparing identity, but even if it's not, it largely just clutters the code. Plus, you never know; your descriptor may be used in place of a special method.

The final result looks like this:

```
def name_of(descriptor, owner):
    return first(attr for attr in dir(owner)
                 if (get_descriptor(owner, attr) is
                 descriptor))

def first(iter):
    return next(iter, None)

def get_descriptor(cls, descname):
    selected_class = first(clss for clss in cls.__mro__
                           if descname in clss.__dict__)
    return selected_class.__dict__[descname]
```

Python 3.2 also added a new function in the inspect module called getattr_static(), which works just like getattr() except that it doesn't activate a descriptor's __get__() method upon lookup. You could replace the call to get_descriptor() with getattr_static() and it would work the same.

__set_name__()

In Python 3.6, something *else* was added that makes fetching the name even easier! Python gained an additional optional method in its protocol: __set_name__(). This new method is called during the creation of a class that contains a descriptor object. Its parameters are self, owner, and name. The first one, self, is super obvious; it's the same first parameter that all methods have. You should recognize the second one, owner, as the class that the descriptor is on. And the last one, name, should also be evident as the name that we're looking for; the name of the variable that the descriptor object is stored on.

Store the Original and the Mangled

When storing the name used for the descriptor, it's often best to store both the original name *and* the mangled name. Keeping the mangled name is obvious, but why in the world would you want to also store the original name? For error messages. If something goes wrong when trying to use your descriptor, you want to at least provide the name of the attribute to the user to get a better idea of where it all went wrong.

Keying on the ID

Another thing that can be done for relatively safe places to store on the instance is to use the id() of the descriptor to generate a location on the instance, somehow. It seems strange, but a non-string *can* be used as the key in an instance dictionary.

Unfortunately, it can only be accessed directly via vars(instance) [id(desc)] and not via dot notation or get/set/hasattr(). This may actually seem like a plus, since it prevents unwanted access to the attribute, but it also messes up dir(instance), which raises an exception when it finds a non-string key.

On the plus side, it's impossible for this location to clash with user-defined attributes, since those must be strings, and this is an integer. But causing dir() to fail is undesirable, so a different solution must be found. Defining a __dir__() method would be overkill and inappropriate in most cases. However, the aggressive programmer could call object.__dir__() and remove the id() from the list before returning it. As stated, however, this is overkill.

A simple solution is to change the ID into a string, i.e. str(id(desc)) instead of just id(desc). This fixes the dir() problem and also opens up the use of get/set/hasattr() while still preventing dot notation access, since it's an invalid Python identifier. The likelihood of name clashes is still extremely low, so this is still an acceptable solution.

Note   An interesting little twist of `str(id(desc))` is to use the hexadecimal value, as `hex(id(desc))` instead of the straight string version of the number, preferably removing `'0x'` at the beginning, such as `hex(id(desc))[2:]`. The benefit of this is that the hex string will generally be shorter, which shortens the time needed to calculate the hash value (which is done on lookup and assignment in `__dict__`) by a tiny bit. Yes, the amount of time needed to calculate the hex value is greater than that of calculating the plain string value, but that only needs to be done once (you can save the hex string to be used later), whereas attribute lookup is likely to happen many times. It's a tiny optimization and may not even be worth noting.

There's no good reason to add acceptable characters to the front of the key in order to support dot notation, since dot notation requires the user to know what the name is going to be ahead of time, which they can't know since the name changes every time the program is run when using `id()` to derive it. There are other restrictions that a consistently-changing key imposes, one of which is that it makes serialization and deserialization (pickling and unpickling, respectively, done with the `pickle` module, are one of those ways, among others) a little more difficult.

If it's desirable to be able to derive some sort of information from the save location, additional information can be added to the key. For example, the descriptor's class name could be added to the front of the key, for example `type(self).__name__ + str(id(self))`. This gives users who use `dir()` to look through the names on the instance some clue as to what that name refers to, especially if there are multiple descriptors that base their name on `id()` on the instance.

Letting the User Take Care Of It

The title of this section may sound like it's about asking the user for the name in the descriptor's constructor, but that's not it at all. Instead, this is referring to the approach `property` uses.

One could say that `property` "cheats" by simply assigning functions that you give it to its different methods. It acts as the ultimate descriptor by being almost infinitely customizable, and that's largely what it is. The biggest descriptor-y thing it can't do is become a non-data descriptor (since it defines all three methods of the descriptor protocol), which is fine, since that doesn't work with the intent anyway. Also, the functions fed to the descriptor don't have easy access to the descriptor's internals, so there's a limit to what can be done there.

Interestingly, a large percentage of descriptors could be written using `property`—and actually work better, since there would be no difficulties in figuring out where to save the data—but it certainly has major setbacks. The biggest of those is the lack of *DRYness* when it comes to reusing the same descriptor idea. (Don't Repeat Yourself; DRYness is the lack of unnecessarily repeated code.) If the same code has to largely be rewritten many times for the same effect with `property`, it should be turned into a custom descriptor that encapsulates the repeated part. Sadly, it isn't likely to be a really easy copy-over because of the fact of storing a value. If the descriptor doesn't need to figure that out, though, which is sometimes the case, then the conversion is much easier.

In summary, `property` is a highly versatile descriptor, and it even makes some things extremely easy (namely the difficult thing this entire chapter was about), but it's not easily reusable. Custom descriptors are the best solution for that, which is why this book exists!

There aren't many use cases out there for recreating "storage" the way that `property` does it, but there are enough use cases for extending what property does in little ways to make it worthwhile to look into.

Metadescriptors

The restrictions of descriptors and their use with classes can be quite the pain, limiting some of the possibilities that could be wanted from descriptors, such as class constants. It turns out that there *is* a way around it, and that solution will be affectionately called metadescriptors in this book (hopefully the idea and name spreads throughout the advanced Python community).

The reason they are called metadescriptors is because the descriptors, instead of being stored on the classes, are stored on metaclasses. This causes metaclasses to take the place of `owner` while classes take the place of `instance`. Technically, that's all there really is to metadescriptors. It's not even required for a descriptor to be specially designed in order for it to be a metadescriptor.

While the idea of metadescriptors is actually pretty simple, the restrictions around metaclasses can make using metadescriptors more difficult. The biggest restriction that must be noted is the fact that no class can be derived from more than one metaclass, whether that is specified directly on the class or having multiple subclasses have different metaclasses. Don't forget that, even if there is no metaclass specified, a class is still being derived from the `type` metaclass.

Because of this, choosing to use metadescriptors must be done with caution. Luckily, if the codebase is following the guideline of preferring composition to inheritance, this is less likely to be a problem.

For a good example of a metadescriptor, check out the `ClassConstant` metadescriptor near the end of the next chapter.

Summary

In this chapter, we looked at a bunch of examples of techniques for storing values in descriptors, including options for storing on the descriptor as well as on the instances themselves. Now that we know the basics that apply to a majority of descriptors, we'll start looking at some other relatively common functionality and how it can be implemented.

CHAPTER 8

Read-Only Descriptors

There are many good uses for read-only—or immutable—property descriptors. In fact, there is a lot to back up the idea of having everything be effectively immutable. Unfortunately, due to Python's inherent lack of being able to make anything *actually* immutable, interpreter optimization isn't one of those possible benefits with Python. (PyPy may be able to make JIT optimizations because of it, but don't take my word for it.)

There are plenty of other benefits to immutability, but those are beyond the scope of this book. The point of this chapter is to show how a descriptor can make instance-level properties be effectively immutable.

A first stab at making a read-only descriptor might be to not give it a __set__() method, but that works only if there's a __delete__() method. If there's no __delete__() method either, it becomes a non-data descriptor. If it's a non-data descriptor and someone assigns to it, then it just creates an instance attribute that overrides the descriptor. This is clearly not what we want.

No, to truly keep users from assigning new values, __set__() is required, but it obviously can't work as normal. So, what can it do? It can raise an exception. AttributeError is probably the best option of the built-in exceptions, but the functionality is almost unique enough to make a custom exception. It's up to you, but the examples use AttributeError.

© Jacob Zimmerman 2018
J. Zimmerman, *Python Descriptors*, https://doi.org/10.1007/978-1-4842-3727-4_8

Now that the attribute can't be changed, how does one supply it with its original value? Trying to send it through the descriptor's constructor would simply end up with the same value for every instance, since the constructor is only called at class creation time. There needs to be some sort of back door. Three different techniques will be discussed: set-once, secret-set, and forced-set.

Set-Once Descriptors

A set-once descriptor is the most restrictive of the three read-only properties in that it most strongly restricts the number of assignments to once per instance under it.

Set-once descriptors work simply by checking whether a value is already set and acting accordingly. If it's already assigned, it raises an exception; if it's not, then it sets it.

For example, this is what the basic __set__() method would look like if the descriptor was using on-descriptor storage in the instance attribute, storage.

```
def __set__(self, instance, value):
    if instance in self.storage:
        raise AttributeError("Cannot set new value on read-only
        property")
    self.storage[instance] = value
```

First, it checks to see if there's already a value set for the instance. If there is, it raises an AttributeError. Otherwise, it sets the value. Simple.

Of the three read-only descriptors, it's also the simplest to use, since it's set the same way descriptors are normally set: using simple assignment. The others each have a roundabout way of getting the value set. Also, because of it having a typical use for setting the value, it's also the easiest to make versatile.

Secret-Set Descriptors

Secret-set descriptors use a "secret" method on the descriptor to initialize the value. The method uses the same parameters as __set__() and sets the value exactly the way __set__() would do with a normal descriptor. But with this technique, the __set__() method just raises an error.

To have access to the secret method, access to the actual descriptor object is needed. With the current general standard of returning self in the __get__() method when no instance is provided, getting the descriptor from the instance is as easy as type(a).x (you could change it to directly use the class name, but that ignores inheritance and makes a little more if you ever refactor the name). Even with returning unbound attributes, this is possible, although it requires an extra step. You may recall that UnboundAttribute has a descriptor attribute of its own. So, the lookup becomes just a little longer. Instead of just type(a).x, it becomes type(a).x.descriptor. Once you have access to the descriptor object, all that needs to be done is call the "secret" set method. Here's an example of a class using a secret-set descriptor called ROValue in the __init__() method.

```
class A:
    val = ROValue()

    def __init__(self, value):
        type(self).val.set(self, value)
```

The descriptor is accessed, then set()—the descriptor's "secret" set method—is called to initialize the value for the instance. This is more verbose than self.val = value, but it works.

In the library, there are some helper functions (some of which are standardized within the library) that can be used. The one that is most guaranteed to work in every case (including instance attributes) is setattribute(instance, attr_name, value). There are also some optional parameters with default values that can be set for specifying the specific behavior, but the defaults will try everything (including techniques not shown here yet) until something works.

Forced-Set Descriptors

The way that forced-set descriptors work is, instead of using an entirely new method as a back door, it still uses __set__(), but with a twist. Instead of just the typical three parameters (self, instance, and value), it has a fourth with a default value. This parameter is something like forced=False. This makes it so that the built-in way of calling __set__() will not cause the value to be set. Rather, the descriptor object needs to be accessed and have __set__() called explicitly with the additional forced=True argument. So, if ROValue was a forced-set descriptor instead the previous secret-set one, the basic __set__() method would look like this:

```
def __set__(self, instance, value, forced=False):
    if not forced:
        raise AttributeError("Cannot set new value on read-only
        property")
    # setter implementation here
```

Now the __set__() method checks whether the forced parameter is set to True. If it's not, then the method fails like any other read-only descriptor should. If it is True, though, then the method knows to let it pass and actually set the value.

If a descriptor is truly only meant to be written to during object creation, using the set-once descriptor is the best choice. It's harder for users of the descriptor to thwart the read-only nature of the set-once descriptor than it is for the other two options. Choosing between either of the other two is a matter of preference. Some may find that altering the signature of a "magic" method doesn't sit well with them, although some may enjoy the lack of a need for another method. Some may actually prefer the additional method, since they may already be using it, as shown in some examples in Chapter 11. For the most part, choosing between the secret-set and forced-set descriptor designs is just about preference.

Class Constants

Class constants are very much like read-only descriptors except that, when done properly, they don't need to be set-once; instead, they're set upon creation. This requires a little bit of tweaking, though.

First, you must realize that a descriptor for a class constant must be implemented as a metadescriptor (in case you forgot, that's a descriptor on the metaclass) instead of a normal one. Second, each class that has constants will likely have its own set of constants, which means each of those classes will need a custom metaclass just for itself.

To begin, here's the actual descriptor that will be used.

```
class Constant:
    def __init__(self, value):
        self.value = value

    def __get__(self, instance, owner):
        return self.value

    def __set__(self, instance, value):
        raise AttributeError("Cannot change a constant")

    def __delete__(self, instance):
        raise AttributeError("Cannot delete a constant")
```

It's an extremely simple descriptor, receiving a value in its constructor, returning it with a __get__() call, and raising an AttributeError if someone attempts to change or delete the value.

To use this descriptor, though, it must be placed in a metaclass, which must then have a class to derive from it. For an example, here is an instance of a metaclass and class holding several mathematical constants.

```
class MathMeta(type):
    PI = Constant(3.14159)
    e = Constant(2.71828)
    GOLDEN_RATIO = Constant(1.61803)

class Math(metaclass=MathMeta):
    pass
```

Now PI, e, and the GOLDEN_RATIO are constants of the Math class. The only way to mess with them is through the metaclass. A downside to using a metadescriptor for this is the fact the constants can no longer be accessed through instances of classes with the constant. This isn't really a problem though, since many other languages never permitted that kind of access to begin with. There are also multiclassing issues that can pop up with classes that have different metaclasses, but that's a pretty rare issue.

So, now that there's a Constant metadescriptor and it's understood how to use it, I will now channel my inner Raymond Hettinger by saying, "There must be a better way!" Nobody wants to make a metaclass just so they can make a normal class have constants.

There *is* a better way. Python allows for dynamically defining classes and metaclasses, and if they're created within a function, that definition can be reused dynamically over and over again. Here's how.

```
def withConstants(**kwargs):
    class MetaForConstants(type):
        pass
    for k, v in kwargs.items():
        MetaForConstants.__dict__[k] = Constant(v)
    return MetaForConstants
```

This function creates a metaclass using each given keyword argument as a new `Constant` and returns the metaclass. Here's what the new `Math` class definition would look like with this function instead of the fully written metaclass.

```
class Math(metaclass=withConstants(PI=3.14159, e=2.71828,
GOLDEN_RATIO=1.61803)):
    pass
```

There! Now, just by setting the resulting metaclass as `Math`'s metaclass, it has the constants provided by the keyword arguments given to `withConstants()`. There is one huge drawback to using this over the other way: autocompletion. You'd be hard pressed to find an editor that can autocomplete on something created completely dynamically like this.

Summary

This chapter has examined several different techniques to make descriptors for read-only attributes (or, at least, read-only-ish attributes). One thing to note in all of this is that none of the techniques actually make it impossible to change the values; they only make it difficult to do so, requiring extra steps in order to signify to the user that doing so is not what was intended. Such is the way of Python; after all, we're all consenting adults here.

CHAPTER 9

Writing __delete__()

This is going to be a short chapter, since there isn't really all that much to say, but it didn't really fit in any of the other chapters. Also, __get__() and __set__() sort of got their own chapters.

Most descriptor tutorials don't even mention what to do with __delete__(), and they often don't even have the method on their example descriptors.

If a descriptor is being used only internally (as opposed to being in a public library) and del is never called in the internal code, then there is no point in implementing a __delete__() method. But in a public library, there is no way to know whether or not users are going to use del on the descriptor attributes. Because of that, it is generally safest to include working __delete__() methods on data descriptors in a library. How those methods look depends on how the attributes are stored.

For internal storage, delete the entry from the dict:

```
del self.storage[instance]
```

For external storage, delete from the instance dictionary:

```
del vars(instance)[name]
```

If the descriptor doesn't represent a stored value, do nothing. There's truly very little variation in what __delete__() methods look like, other than the additional functionality a descriptor may have.

© Jacob Zimmerman 2018
J. Zimmerman, *Python Descriptors*, https://doi.org/10.1007/978-1-4842-3727-4_9

Summary

We've seen that __delete__() is a pretty simple method to implement, but deciding whether to actually implement it can be a difficult decision. In the end, though, it will be used so little that implementing it can probably be put off until it's needed. The default behavior of raising an exception due to lack of implementation should get you by until then.

CHAPTER 10

Descriptors Are Classes Too

It's time for some more advanced stuff with descriptors. Actually, it's not really advanced, since it's stuff that pertains to all classes. There won't be a very in-depth look at much in this chapter; it's just a reminder that features normally available to classes are available to descriptors as well.

Inheritance

Descriptors can inherit and be inherited from other classes (which will generally be other descriptors or descriptor utilities/helpers). Using inheritance, descriptors can be built using pre-built mixins and template classes that already implement the base functionality wanted for storing the attribute. In fact, a suite of these are discussed in the next chapter and fully provided in the library. Just as an example, a base class can be created that takes care of the minor details of using on-descriptor storage that the derived specialization can delegate to. Again, there's more about this idea in the next chapter, with full code examples in the library.

© Jacob Zimmerman 2018

J. Zimmerman, *Python Descriptors*, https://doi.org/10.1007/978-1-4842-3727-4_10

More Methods

A descriptor can have more methods than just that of the descriptor protocol, __set_name__(), and __init__(). This was shown with secret-set descriptors that have a back door method, like set().

Externally-used methods like that should be limited, since access to these methods should be limited too, but using internally-used "private" methods that are used only within the class are definitely fair game. Also, implementing __str__() and __repr__() is a good idea too. It's rarely useful or necessary to implement __eq__() or __hash__(), as descriptors themselves aren't likely compared or stored in a hashed collection as a key.

Optional/Default Parameters

Just like in the forced-set descriptors, optional/default parameters can be added to the protocol methods. Since users providing alternative arguments still requires them to get the descriptor object and call the protocol methods directly, this should be limited, just like additional externally-used methods.

Additionally, it should be limited for the sake of composition and inheritance. If the class providing the optional parameter gets wrapped or subclassed, the new class either has to know about the optional parameter or provide a **kwargs parameter and pass it down the line, as will be seen in much of the provided code in the library.

Descriptors on Descriptors

Since descriptors are classes, descriptors can have descriptors on them too! There have been several times that I almost did so, but the setter was more complicated than what descriptors provide, so I had to settle. I've also considered using descriptors to make the attributes read-only, but I've never fully settled on it.

Passing an Instance Around

No one ever said that a descriptor had to create a new instance for each and every class it was put on. An instance of a descriptor can be created outside of a class definition, then assigned to a class attribute of multiple classes.

This can save a little bit of space when storing on the descriptor, since it will only have the overhead of a single dictionary instead of one per class. In fact, if you're storing the values on the descriptor, it's much less of a problem than saving on the instance. The issue with descriptors storing the values on the instance is that you need the name to store it on, and if that name is supposed to the same as or derived from the name the descriptor has on the class, you have to deal with the possibility that the descriptor has multiple names. Interestingly, __set_name__() is called each time you assign the descriptor to a class in the class definition. If you don't need the name (you should, for error messages), you can still get away with a single descriptor used on multiple classes. The best use case is when the descriptor is really specific and used with the same name on every class. This eliminates all of the problems.

But if you want to use a single instance of a descriptor across multiple classes that can potentially use a different name for it, you'll need to create a specialized storage for those names that is keyed by classes, but can also take inheritance into account. I would actually enjoy the challenge and have considered creating one to put into descriptor-tools, but I don't want to encourage the idea too much.

Whatever you do, do not reuse the same descriptor for multiple attributes on the same class. It simply won't work. All the attributes will have the same value.

Descriptors Just Abstract Method Calls

Basically, a descriptor is just a simpler way to do certain method calls. Those method calls don't *have* to work in a `property`-ish way, getting and/or setting a certain value.

The __get__() descriptor method can essentially replace any method on a class that takes no parameters and returns an object. What's more, it doesn't even need to return anything, since not returning anything means it returns None. The __set__() descriptor method can be a replacement for any method that has a single parameter and doesn't return anything. The __delete__() method replaces methods with no parameters and doesn't return anything.

While a descriptor *can* be used in these ways, doing so is very likely to be unintuitive to users of the descriptor, largely due to the fact that the syntax seems strange for many of those cases, especially in the case of __delete__().

Summary

Anything that can be done with any other class can be done with a descriptor, including things not brought up here. Although much of it *can* be done without any real downsides, there is rarely a need for many of the features, but it doesn't hurt to keep all of this in mind when writing your descriptors.

CHAPTER 11

Reusing the Wheel

Whenever possible and sensible, one should try to avoid reinventing the wheel. This chapter goes over a set of classes to use as superclasses and strategies to help build new descriptors a little faster. Only barebones code is presented here; the full code examples are in the library.

Storage Solutions

The first code examples cover storage "strategies" (which I'm calling "solutions") that a descriptor can use for its storage. These strategies can be hard-coded into new descriptors or be passed into the descriptor's initializer to be chosen on a case-by-case basis. Only two basic strategies will be shown here; the rest can be found in the library.

```python
class OnDescriptorStorageSolution:
    def __init__(self):
        self.storage = DescriptorStorage()

    def get(self, instance):
        return self.storage[instance]

    def set(self, instance, value):
        self.storage[instance] = value

    def delete(self, instance):
        del self.storage[instance]
```

© Jacob Zimmerman 2018
J. Zimmerman, *Python Descriptors*, https://doi.org/10.1007/978-1-4842-3727-4_11

```
class NameGetter:
    def __init__(self, name_lookup_strategy):
        self.lookup_strategy = name_lookup_strategy
        self.name = None

    def __call__(self, instance, descriptor):
        if self.name is None:
            self.name = self.lookup_strategy(instance,
            descriptor)
        return self.name

    def set(self, name):
        self.name = name

class OnInstanceStorageSolution:
    def __init__(self, name_lookup_strategy):
        self.name = NameGetter(name_lookup_strategy)

    def get(self, instance):
        return instance.__dict__[self.name(instance, self)]

    def set(self, instance, value):
        instance.__dict__[self.name(instance, self)] = value

    def delete(self, instance):
        del instance.__dict__[self.name(instance, self)]

    def set_name(self, name):
        self.name.set(name)
```

Clearly, these storage solutions are designed for per-instance storage. This is due to two reasons: per-class storage is trivial and therefore doesn't need pre-built solutions; and per-instance storage is much more common.

The NameGetter class and its use might be just a little confusing. As stated in the chapter about storage, the most difficult thing about storing on the instances is figuring out how to find the name of where to store, so the

OnInstanceStorageSolution class takes in a name_lookup_strategy. This strategy is just a function that accepts instance and the descriptor and returns the name to store at. The strategy accepts those two parameters because those are the only pieces of information guaranteed that can be used for the lookup, and they're also required for doing lookup via name_of(), as mentioned earlier in the book. If the name is already decided, the lookup strategy can simply be None, and you call set(). The set() method is also useful for being called from __set_name__(), which is why OnInstanceStorageSolution also has a set_name() method to be called from the descriptor.

NameGetter isn't technically required to do the work necessary, but is used to cache the name after the name has been calculated. That way, the lookup method doesn't need to be called more than once; it's called once, then stored for quick returns on subsequent lookups.

Now that storage solutions have been shown, here are some example descriptors using or prepared to be supplied with a storage solution object (delete methods are omitted for simplicity's sake).

```
class ExampleWithHardCodedStrategy:
    def __init__(self):
        self.storage = OnDescriptorStorageSolution()

    def __get__(self, instance, owner):
        # any pre-fetch logic
        value = self.storage.get(instance)
        # any post-fetch logic
        return value

    def __set__(self, instance, value):
        # any pre-set logic
        self.storage.set(instance, value)

class ExampleWithOpenStrategy:
    def __init__(self, storage_solution):
        self.storage = storage_solution
```

```
def __get__(self, instance, owner):
    # any pre-fetch logic
    value = self.storage.get(instance)
    # any post-fetch logic
    return value

def __set__(self, instance, value):
    # any pre-set logic
    self.storage.set(instance, value)
```

These strategies could also be subclassed, making the strategy methods more like template-called methods. For example:

```
class ExampleWithSuperclassStrategy(OnDescriptorStorageSolution):
    def __get__(self, instance, owner):
        # any pre-fetch logic
        value = self.get(instance) # calls the solution method
        on itself
        # any post-fetch logic
        return value

    def __set__(self, instance, value):
        # any pre-set logic
        self.set(instance, value) # same here
```

Using the storage solutions like this is a cleaner way of hard-coding the solution.

Read-Only Solutions

Another utility class that can be built is a wrapper that can turn *any* other descriptor into a read-only descriptor. Here's an example using the set-once style.

```
class ReadOnly:
    def __init__(self, wrapped):
        self.wrapped = wrapped
        self.setInstances = set()

    def __set__(self, instance, value):
        if instance in self.setInstances:
            raise AttributeError("Cannot set new value on read-
            only property")
        else:
            self.setInstances.add(instance)
            self.wrapped.__set__(instance, value)

    def __getattr__(self, item):
        # redirects any calls other than __set__ to the wrapped
        descriptor
        return getattr(self.wrapped, item)

def readOnly(deco):  # a decorator for wrapping other decorator
descriptors
    def wrapper(func):
        return ReadOnly(deco(func))
    return wrapper
```

It even includes a decorator decorator for decorating descriptors being used as decorators. (Yo dawg; I heard you like decorators, so I put decorators in your decorators.) This isn't meant for wrapping just any decorators; it's only meant for wrapping decorators that produce descriptors. It's not likely to be used often, since most descriptors that are created from decorators are non-data descriptors, making the ReadOnly wrapping not very useful. But it doesn't hurt to have it anyway, just in case; especially after claiming it can wrap *any* other descriptor.

It can be noted that ReadOnly only implements the __set__() method of the descriptor protocol. This is because it's the only one that it covers. It uses __getattr__() in order to redirect calls to potential __get__() and __delete__() methods because it doesn't know which ones might be implemented. Unfortunately, this doesn't work. When calling "magic" methods implicitly, Python doesn't look up the methods normally. For the sake of speed, it directly checks just the dictionary on the classes and no further.

This unfortunately makes using the object-oriented decorator pattern extremely difficult to do correctly. Essentially, you need to implement the methods in such a way as to mimic __getattribute__() itself. In descriptor_tools.decorators.DescriptorDecoratorBase, you can see what I mean. It checks what methods the wrapped descriptor has and decides whether to delegate to the wrapped descriptor, to the instance, or to raise errors you'd otherwise get.

An alternative is to design your descriptors to take strategies at creation, but this only works with your own descriptors and doesn't allow you to extend descriptors that are out of your control.

Simple Unbound Attributes

Reusable code can be created for making the __get__() method return unbound attributes when instance isn't provided rather than returning the descriptor, too. It can be done via a wrapper class (assuming it's designed to handle the correct methods), via inheritance, or even a method decorator:

```
def binding(get):
    @wraps(get)
    def wrapper(self, instance, owner):
        if instance is None:
            return UnboundAttribute(self, owner)
```

```
        else:
            return get(self, instance, owner)
    return wrapper
```

This simple decorator can be used inside a descriptor easily:

```
class Descriptor:
    # other implementation details
    @binding
    def __get__(self, instance, owner):
        # implementation that assumes instance is not None
```

By simply adding the call to the decorator, you can simplify the code you have to write, ignoring writing anything that has to deal with the possibility of instance being None, other than the decorator.

There's also an object decorator (i.e., a Gang of Four decorator) version in the library so that any existing descriptor can be transformed to return unbound attributes. For example, if users want to use attribute binding with an existing descriptor that doesn't provide them, they could do something like this:

```
class MyClass:
    @Binding
    @property
    def myProp(self):
        # gets the actual property
```

Binding is a class that wraps an entire descriptor. Now property can be used with unbound attributes. (With some caveats: if you continue and define a setter for myProp, myProp will be replaced with a *new* property object; only add the @Binding call to the *last* method decorated with the property.) With descriptors that aren't being used as decorators, it would look like this:

```
class MyClass:
    myProp = Binding(SomeDescriptor(...))
```

There is no version that works with inheritance since calling either of the decorators is easier than trying to create a superclass for the new descriptor to inherit from.

Summary

This is all the categories of helpful code provided in the library (other than what the entire next chapter is about), but it is by no means the only pieces of code there. There are a ton of helpful pieces there to help you build your own descriptors, to mix and match certain pieces into a cohesive whole descriptor where you need to do minimal work to add your core logic among the rest of it.

In this chapter, we've seen how reusable pieces can be made that can make implementing descriptors a little quicker and easier, as well as a little bit more standardized. As mentioned, all of these tools (and more) will be available in the library as well as on GitHub. Hopefully, they will help make your lives easier when you try to create your own descriptors.

CHAPTER 12

Instance-Level Descriptors

What's the most confusing part about a property-like data descriptor? Wrapping your head around the fact that it is being used to control instance-distinct attributes from its class.

What's the hardest decision you have to make? Whether to store on the descriptor or on the instance (and then how you plan to accomplish that).

With instance properties, these issues are delegated to a nano framework so that you can concentrate on the important parts of your descriptor, creating a property that works the way you'd expect. Let's get a little history to understand what I'm talking about.

Properties in Other Languages

When you see properties in other languages, such as C#, those properties work a lot like methods in that they're defined on the class, but you get to focus on the instance while you're working. In fact, they're defined very much like methods and probably have the same or a similar implementation in the back.

Python's `property` descriptor allows you to do something very similar, albeit in a slightly more verbose and unintuitive way, but you can still do it.

Next, we'll look at Kotlin, which allows you to define properties in much the same way as C#, but they also have a secondary system called

© Jacob Zimmerman 2018
J. Zimmerman, *Python Descriptors*, https://doi.org/10.1007/978-1-4842-3727-4_12

delegated properties. This is where you provide the property definition with an object that has get() and set() methods. Does this sound familiar? Sounds a lot like descriptors, right? There's one big difference, though: there's one delegated property object per instance. This makes it so that the delegated property only has to worry about what it's doing with each instance. It also means that, since a new property is created with each instance, it can take a starting value in its constructor and never implement a set() method if it wants to be read-only; it doesn't need set() to give it its first value. This is so much nicer than Python's descriptors in most cases.

Back to Python

Now, don't get me wrong; Python's descriptors are an amazing feature, and the fact that they reside at the class level opens up a whole new world of possibilities. But the problem is that, arguably, most use cases for descriptors don't need that. In fact, I would venture that most of the time, people just want a reusable property.

So, what can we do about this? We can make our own delegated properties, of course!

Accomplishing this went through at least four different iterations for me, starting off with using a completely different kind of Python metaprogramming. You can see the first two attempts on my blog, "Programming Ideas with Jake," under my articles about descriptors.

Attempt 1

The first thing I tried was a more direct manipulation of how Python classes work to look and act more like it does in Kotlin. When you first set the attribute on an instance that you wanted with a delegated property, you assigned it an instance of that delegated property object. Then you would tweak __getattribute__() and __setattr__() so that if the attribute held a delegated property, it would call the appropriate method on it instead. Reusing the tweaked version of the __getattribute__() and __setattr__() could be done fairly easily with inheritance or a class decorator that does monkey patching.

As well as this works, it doesn't sit well with me because I hate messing with those attribute access hooks. It seems *too* magical to me.

Attempt 2

I believe I was lying in bed about to fall asleep, when this idea came to me, causing me to stay up a little longer while I wrote it down. The idea was half-baked at first, but the basics of it run the rest of the attempts. Then, as I started to write it in code, I started to see certain issues and came up with a situation that will probably make you think of some jokes about Java frameworks.

The basics of the idea is that, instead of tweaking the attribute access methods, we move those changes out into a descriptor. That descriptor is called with any and all uses of its attribute, where it delegates to a delegated property object. It's a pretty simple base of an idea.

From there, the problem came down to one question: how do we instantiate the delegated property instances? You may or may not already have a good guess, and the part that made my life so difficult was the idea that I thought the framework had to work in a way such that everything about the property had to be defined in that initial line on the class, and the constructor pretty much just needed to provide the starting value.

So the descriptor needed to be constructed with a factory function for creating the delegated property. But I also wanted to make it so that the delegated property could:

- Be created without a value initially. For example, a lazy attribute where the lazy initialization function is provided with the factory. Or a property that can't be None but might not have a value initially.

- Could skip implementing the setter method to be read-only.

- Could potentially take in some metadata, such as its name as well as what instance it's for.

To do this, the first time the attribute was accessed, the descriptor created a blank version of the delegated property object and passed it and the metadata in an "InstancePropertyInitializer," which had an `initialize()` method that you had to call in your normal constructor. This initializer method delegated to the `initialize()` method on the delegated property, sending in the metadata and whatever else the developer wanted to send into the property. The existence and flexibility of that initializer is what allowed delegated properties to accomplish this list of possibilities. If you don't want an initial value, then just don't give one to the initializer. If you want to skip having the setter method for a read-only property (but the framework can't provide the initial value in the constructor), the initializer acts like a special backdoor setter. It's also the vehicle for supplying the metadata.

The idea seemed pretty elegant to me at the time, but it dawned on me how cumbersome it was. First, the delegated property needed to provide an initializer method, plus it needed to provide a factory method. Also, initializing the attribute was weird, looking like `self.attr.initialize(value)` instead of just `self.attr = value`.

Attempt 3

Then, while I was on a camping trip and starting to work on my edits for this new edition, a better idea came to me. It followed mostly the same idea, but it made it nicer for properties that were given a starting value in the constructor.

To do this, the factory was changed to take in the metadata as well as an initial value. Now the delegated property could take in all of those things in the constructor. So, the first time that the attribute is set, the descriptor creates the property with all of that. This allowed the constructor code to go back to the `self.attr = value` format.

But what about ones that don't want an initial value? Those classes have to take an extra step. Their factories had to have a `default()` method that on took in the metadata. This would be called if the delegated property still hadn't been created for an instance but the descriptor's `__get__()` method was being called. From there, the descriptor could start delegating to the property.

The reason that we have a default factory that is different than the normal factory is because most properties that would use a default factory also still allow the value to be initialized first.

Attempt 4

Before I was even done with that camping trip, I realized how dumb I had been all along and started work on this fourth, and hopefully final, attempt. We don't need factories. Instead, at the class level, all you do is create the base `InstanceProperty` descriptor (shown below). The descriptor is just there to activate that attribute to use delegated properties. It simply assumes that the first assignment to the attribute is assigning the property itself instead of just a value. The descriptor doesn't need to know what kind of property it will be storing or how to create it.

Instead, you create the delegate property instance in the class' constructor. This has the added benefit of making sure that, if the descriptor stores the delegated property on the instance, the property is assigned in the constructor, which is recommended in Python 3.3+ due to key-sharing dictionaries. Sure, it's no longer self.attr = value. Now it's self.attr = PropertyType(value), which is more cumbersome but doesn't feel nearly as weird, and it allows the design of the delegated property types to be notably easier.

There is still one awkward thing that needs to be dealt with on the property class. It needs a method for providing the metadata. It's either do that or cause the attribute initialization line to look like self.attr = PropertyType(value, self, "attr", type(self).attr), assuming the property wants all three pieces of metadata (the instance, the attribute name, and the descriptor the property is controlled by).

So what does this descriptor look like? Here's a simplified version:

```python
class InstanceProperty:
    def __init__(self):
        self._storage = DescDict()

    def __set_name__(self, owner, name):
        self._name = name

    def __get__(self, instance, owner):
        if instance is None:
            return self
        else:
            return self._storage[instance].get()

    def __set__(self, instance, value):
        if instance not in self._storage:
            value.set_meta(instance, self._name, self)
            self._storage[instance] = value
```

```
    else:
        self._storage[instance].set(value)

def __delete__(self, instance):
    del self._storage[instance]
```

The real one that's included in the descriptor-tools library in version
1.1 (still unreleased at the time of writing) has more to it, allowing for
the name to be set in versions that don't support __set_name__(). The
real one also makes the properties not deletable by default (a Deletable
wrapper allows it) and allows you to use a simple wrapper for the
descriptor that makes it read-only so that you don't have create a mutable
and read-only version of the delegated properties.

Example

I'm betting you want to see all of this in action, don't you? We'll create a
delegated property that doesn't allow the attribute to be None:

```
class NotNone:
    def __init__(self, value):
        self.value = value

    def set_meta(self, instance, name, descriptor):
        self.instance = instance
        self.name = name
        self.descriptor = descriptor
        if value is None:
            raise AttributeError(self.name + "cannot be None")

    def get(self):
        return self.value
```

```
def set(self, value):
    if value is None:
        raise AttributeError(self.name + "cannot be None")
    else:
        self.value = value
```

This example also shows a small inconvenience with the framework: if you want a property that does some kind of validation and wants to use any of the metadata in the error message, you need to wait until set_meta() to do the initial validation. From the user's perspective, this is effectively at the exact same point in time, but it's awkward from the perspective of the person who has to write the property.

But you know what else this example shows? It shows how simple and intuitive the rest of creating a delegated property can be.

So what does it look like to use all of this?

```
class Foo:
    bar = InstanceAttribute()

    def __init__(self, baz):
        self.bar = NotNone(baz)

    ...
```

Just a little bit of extra work for a clean and easy way to have special attributes.

Go Nuts

While there is a default option for an instance attribute descriptor coming to descriptor-tools, that was designed to be as general as I knew how to make it. If you don't care at all about the metadata, you can create your own instance attribute descriptor and strip that whole bit out. You're nearly done with this book; you've got this!

CHAPTER 13

Other Uses of Descriptors In the World

Much of the usefulness of descriptors covered in this book was just using them as specialized properties. While this is one of the primary purposes of descriptors, it's not all that they can do, though even the more innovative uses still largely serve that purpose.

SQLAlchemy[4]

This is probably the best-known library that uses descriptors for some of its stronger powers. (Probably; I did some digging and couldn't find any hint of using descriptors, though the inheritance hierarchy is deep, so I gave up. If it *doesn't* use descriptors, then I have absolutely no clue how it does what it does.) When using the declarative mapping style for data classes, the use of the Column descriptor allows users to specify all sorts of database metadata about the column that the attribute represents, including the data type, column name, whether it's a primary key, etc.

That Column class also has a ton of other methods that are used when creating queries around the data, such as the ordering methods, __lt__(), __gt__(), etc. and what table it's in.

© Jacob Zimmerman 2018
J. Zimmerman, *Python Descriptors*, https://doi.org/10.1007/978-1-4842-3727-4_13

Jigna

Jigna is a library that provides a kind of bridge between Python and JavaScript, allowing you to write Python code that creates web pages, including single-page applications. Using Trait descriptors, it can create two-way data bindings, generating AngularJS code that works with HTML pages.

The use is extremely innovative and powerful and it's all thanks to descriptors that it can be as easy to use as it is.

For more information, visit its GitHub repository[5] or check out the presentation the creator gave at EuroPython 2014[6].

Elk

Elk is a Python library that is almost all descriptors, allowing for classes to be defined in a stricter fashion. Every attribute for instances is meant to be defined in the class with an `ElkAttribute` descriptor. Some examples of what can be done with `ElkAttributes` are:

- Setting an attribute as required

- Making lazy attributes

- Delegating to the methods on the attribute

- Making an attribute read-only

- Creating constructors automatically

There are other features in the library attempting to make the tedious parts of class definition a little easier, and they can be seen in its documentation[7].

Validators

This isn't a specific instance of what's out there, but rather a well-known use for descriptors. For example, if an attribute needs to be a string that follows a certain pattern, a descriptor can be created that takes the validator, and every time a value is set into the descriptor, it validates that the new value fits the validation.

There are a bunch of different validation descriptors that can be written that allow a class to maintain its invariants.

Summary

Now you've seen some really cool uses for descriptors. Also, this is the end of the book, so I suggest you go out there and make your own really awesome descriptors. Go and make the Python community an even more awesome place.

Bibliography

1. GitHub repo of descriptor tools https://github.com/sad2project/descriptor-tools

2. Python documentation on property http://tinyurl.com/ljsmxck

3. "The Zipline Show" about descriptors https://www.youtube.com/watch?v=xYBVjVEJtEg

4. SQLAlchemy site http://www.sqlalchemy.org/

5. Jigna GitHub repo https://github.com/enthought/jigna

6. Jigna presentation at EuroPython 2014 https://www.youtube.com/watch?v=KHSXq5jfv_4

7. Elk documentation http://frasertweedale.github.io/elk/

J. Zimmerman, *Python Descriptors*, https://doi.org/10.1007/978-1-4842-3727-4

Index

J. Zimmerman, *Python Descriptors*, https://doi.org/10.1007/978-1-4842-3727-4

E, F

G, H

I

J

K, L

Printed in the United States
By Bookmasters